The
Christmas
Cookie
Tree

The Christmas Cookie Tree

Written and Illustrated by

RUTH HERSHEY IRION

j

THE WESTMINSTER PRESS
Philadelphia

The illustrations in this book are created in the manner of Pennsylvania Dutch *Fraktur* art—decorative writing and design used from about 1750 to 1850 to record events in Pennsylvania Dutch life.

The design motifs are authentic.

"Still Six More

days till Christmas."
Eva counted on her fingers.
"Six long, long days!"

She stood at her bedroom window and stared out
beyond the big horse chestnut tree in the yard. The
bare apple trees on the hill looked like twisted black
crayon marks on the white snow. They look just like I
feel, she thought—lonely and bent out of shape.

All the excitement of moving was over. Philadelphia was miles away. It was so strange here. So quiet.
So different.

"And even Christmas will be different," Eva sighed, turning from the window.

She left her room and went downstairs, dragging her feet. From the hall she could hear her parents talking in the kitchen. She stopped in the doorway.

Mr. Moyer was saying, "I tell you, Mary, it's like slipping into a comfortable pair of old shoes to be here. It's great, living in the country again after all these years." He leaned back in his chair.

"Yes, it is, Dan—for you and me," said Mrs. Moyer. She drank the last drop of her coffee. "But I'm not so sure about Evie. It's such a big change from city life. Evie may find it's more like a new pair of shoes—tight new shoes that pinch." She set her coffee cup down.

Eva walked slowly into the kitchen.

"Pick up your feet, Evie. Don't drag them so." Her mother looked over at her anxiously.

"You still a puss in a strange garret, Puss?" Mr. Moyer said when he saw her long face.

Eva gave him a thin smile and sat down on her chair.

Mrs. Moyer started to clear the table. "Guess I should've used Great Granny's old recipe for moving," she said.

Eva looked up quickly. "Is there a *recipe* for moving, Mom?"

"Great Granny had a recipe," her mother answered. "She called moving into a new house a 'flitting.' She used to say, 'When you have a flitting, send a broom and a loaf of bread on ahead and you won't get homesick.' "

"Such nonsense!" Mr. Moyer reached for his boots and pulled them on. "Well, I must be off to the barn."

He stopped by Eva's chair and patted her on the head. "Cheer up, Puss—Christmas is coming!"

Eva wrinkled her nose. She wasn't sure that Christmas would help. Not this year.

As Mr. Moyer passed his wife, he pinched her cheek. "And your Great Granny might have said, 'A fat wife and a full barn never did any man harm.' "

"Out with you, Dan!" Mrs. Moyer tossed her head. "I'm not fat, and your barn's not full yet!" But she laughed as he left.

Eva kicked her shoe against the table leg.

Turning from the sink, her mother said, "Evie, put

your wraps on now and take these change-of-address cards out to the mailbox for me."

Eva walked slowly out of the house and down the path. She kicked the snow all the way to the tall mailbox. Even the mailbox was different. It was made of tin and nailed to the top of an old wooden fence post. She could barely reach it. Standing on tiptoes, she tugged at the drop-down door. It was frozen shut.

She made a fist of her mittened hand and pounded around the icy edges. She tugged again with all her might. With a loud cracking noise the ice broke away. The door fell open.

"Hallo! *Kannscht du Deitsch schwetza?*" said a strange voice.

Eva turned with a start, dropping the cards.

A red-faced jolly-looking man leaned out from the window of his car.

"Ach, I didn't mean to scare you, yet," he said. He opened the car door and stepped out to help her pick up the cards.

"Oh, you didn't scare me. It's just that I didn't hear you come." Eva picked up a card. "I was busy knocking the ice off the mailbox door."

The man nodded. "Yah, and the roads are quiet still, when the snow lies yet so thick."

Eva straightened up and looked at him. "What did you say to me a minute ago that sounded so funny?"

"I just asked, *Kannscht du Deitsch schwetza?*"

"Kans do—What?"

The man roared with laughter. "Oh ho! A little *Auslander* yet! *Kannscht du Deitsch schwetza* just says, 'Can you talk Dutch?' But I see you don't. You must come from the Outside."

"We moved here last Tuesday from Philadelphia," Eva said.

"Oh? It wondered me where the folks who moved into the old Scheaffer place come from," the man said. "Philadelphia, yet? The Big City?"

Eva nodded. "Yes. But you know what? Sometimes my daddy teases me with funny-sounding words like you just said. He told me our neighbors here could speak Pennsylvania Dutch. Are you a neighbor?" she asked.

"Not such a near neighbor. I live in town. I'm just the old mailman."

"Mailman!" Eva looked at him in disbelief. She stared at his car. The front seat was filled with bundles of letters and newspapers. The back seat was covered with packages. She looked at the man who held her cards in his hand. He looked just like anyone else—no blue uniform, no special hat. "You're not like our mailman in the city!" she said.

"Yah well, country ways are different still, but mailman I am." He climbed back into his car. He closed the door. Then he rolled down his window. "What's your name, yet?" he asked.

"Eva. Eva Moyer."

"That's sure a good enough Dutch-sounding name," he said. "I come back again tomorrow. I fetch you some mail then maybe."

Eva didn't want him to go. He was the first person she had met in this new countryside.

"Do you always speak Pennsylvania Dutch?" She looked up at him.

"I talk Dutch when I talk to the Dutch. I talk English when I talk to the *Auslanders*," he grinned at her. "I talk three languages yet—English, Dutch, and Dumb!" He raced the motor of his car, laughing loudly at the joke on himself. Then he leaned out of the window. "I must get off now if I am to get myself done, with all this Christmas mail to cart around."

Eva giggled. "Maybe I'll see you again."

"Sure now," he waved as he drove away.

Eva raced to the old stone farmhouse and burst in through the door. Her father was back from the barn, helping her mother unpack the last boxes. They both looked up as she slammed the door behind her.

"Whatever took you so long, Evie?" said her mother.

"And where have you been?" added her father.

Eva started to talk so fast her words tumbled all over each other.

"Whoa! Whoa! Whoa! Slow down," her father said. "Now start all over again, Snicklefritz."

Eva took a big breath and told them all about the mailman. From the beginning.

"He sounds like a lot of the good Dutchmen I grew up with," her father said. "And that reminds me, Puss. It's time you are getting to know your neighbors. I hear they are having a Christmas program down at the old country church. I met the minister in town yesterday, and he said you should come down to their practice tonight."

"No joke, Daddy?" Eva felt all excited.

"No joke, Puss," he smiled at her.

That night Eva and her father drove down to the church, two farms away. The church was buzzing like a beehive. Children were giggling and squirming in the front pews. In the pews behind them, waiting mothers gossiped. And in the very back a small group of men sat, exchanging news.

"What do I do now, Daddy?" Eva gripped his hand tightly.

"See that group of youngsters your size, sitting up front?" he whispered. "I'm sure that's where you belong. I'll sit with the men in the back and wait for you."

Eva walked slowly toward the front of the church.

One end of a pew was empty. She slipped in there and sat down. Two girls, with their heads bent over an open hymnbook, whispered to each other. Eva looked closely at the bigger girl. She had lively brown eyes, and she laughed a lot.

Then she noticed two boys at the end of the pew, wiggling and punching each other. A big girl leaned over the back and forced them apart.

"You are making too much noise, still!" she hissed at them. "Such roughhousing is for the outside! Mind your manners now, or I'll fetch you a good knock on the noggin if you don't look out!"

Both boys slumped down in their seats. Hands thrust in their pockets, they stared straight ahead. Eva watched their restless feet kicking the back of the pew.

Suddenly one boy turned his head and met her gaze. Eva smiled, but he dropped his eyes quickly. His face reddened. He leaned over and poked his friend and whispered to him. The friend stole a glance at Eva. He too looked quickly away. Soon other children were turning and staring at her. But no one returned her smile. Not even the girl with the nice face and the lively brown eyes. They only giggled and whispered among themselves.

Eva felt a hard, choking knot in her chest. She wanted so badly to have them talk to her. Would they be like this when she started to school after Christmas? Would they ever be her friends?

All at once the children stood up and walked away from her. Lost in her loneliness, Eva had not heard the minister's wife tell them to come up. Eva looked after them with the awful feeling that they had guessed her thoughts.

But the minister's wife was motioning to her. "You come along too," she called.

Everyone was looking at Eva and snickering. Trying to make herself as small as possible, she hurried to join the group.

The children swayed back and forth, repeating together in singsong voices their part of the program.

"What shall I give Him, poor as I am?
If I were a shepherd, I'd give Him a lamb.
If I were a Wise Man, I'd do my part.
Yet what shall I give Him? Give Him my heart."

The minister's wife held up her hands. "Now remember, children, the night of the program you bring

your gifts to the baby Jesus just as the shepherds and the Wise Men did. Then you will come over here"—she pointed to the railing in front of the pulpit—"and wait quietly in line to say your piece. On Christmas Day, the minister will take your gifts to the orphanage for the children who have no families to give them a merry Christmas."

Eva wondered what she could bring. What was a good enough gift for the baby Jesus—the baby Jesus who gave Christmas to them all?

Eva sat quietly on the ride back to their new home. Her father chatted about the farms around them, what the farmers grew, and how he couldn't wait to get out and prune the apple trees in the new orchard. And wasn't it great that they were all settled? All ready to get on with their new life?

Eva managed a small, "Yes, Daddy." The lonely knot in her chest felt as big as if she had swallowed whole a round, hard apple.

Eva woke the next morning to the sound of birds. She jumped out of bed and ran to the window. The birds were in the big horse chestnut tree in the yard.

She watched a redheaded woodpecker zip up and down the tree trunk, like a yo-yo on a string, searching the bark for food. Birds hopped in the branches above him, pecking and preening. They twittered. They chirped and whistled as they puffed up their feathers to keep out the cold.

Eva shivered. The chattering of the birds made her think of the chattering children at the church last night—the children who didn't smile at her. The children who laughed at her mistake.

She didn't want to think of them. Quickly she dressed and ran downstairs. She found her mother alone in the kitchen.

"Where's Dad?" she asked.

"He was up and out early this morning," Mrs. Moyer answered. She dished up Eva's breakfast. "He was so excited after talking to the other farmers last night that he had to go right out and inspect his apple trees."

Eva was not hungry for her breakfast. She ate it very slowly.

"What a poke you are this morning, Evie," her mother said. "Did you get out on the wrong side of the bed?"

Eva shook her head. How could she explain that her food stuck in her throat because of the lump in her chest? She looked over at her mother and begged, "Mommie, would you tell me a story?"

"I'll tell you a story," Mrs. Moyer said as she rinsed the glasses, "About Mary Morry.

> And now my story's begun.
> I'll tell you another
> About her brother
> And now my story is done."

"Oh no!" Eva cried impatiently. "That's no story—that's a trick! Please tell me a *real* one—one about when you were young."

"Aren't you getting too big a girl for stories?" her mother said.

"But I just *feel* like a story, Mom. There's nothing else to do right now," Eva pouted.

"Sure there is," Mrs. Moyer said. "You can give me a hand with the dishes or you can take the last of our Christmas cards out for the mailman. It should be about time for him to come."

Eva put on her warm clothing, eager to see the mailman again. She stood down by the tall mailbox and waited for him. Soon she saw his car chugging around the bend.

The mailman slowed to a stop. "*Gooda moria,* good morning," he greeted her cheerily, taking her cards and handing her some mail.

"*Gooda–mor-yah,*" Eva tried. They both laughed.

"Ach, you do so good," the mailman said, "we'll make a little Dutchess of you yet. Yah, I think that's just what I'll call you—Dutchess. How would you like that?"

"Oh, it's just wonderful!" Eva was delighted. She liked having lots of names, and "Dutchess" made her feel warm inside—not quite so strange.

"Well now, you have a name, and my handle is Dietrich. We're all acquainted now, yah? So—how is my *shana* Dutchess?—that means my pretty Dutchess—this morning?"

A little frown pricked Eva's forehead. "Not very well, thank you. I asked my mother to tell me a story, and do you know what she said?—

"I'll tell you a story
About Mary Morry.

And now my story's begun.
I'll tell you another
About her brother
And now my story is done!''

"That's *nothing!*" Eva sputtered.

"Yah well, I too know one that my mother used to tell me when I was a sprout." The mailman leaned out of the window as if to share a secret with Eva. "Listen once. This is a story about a short skirt, Dutchess." Then he whispered in her ear, "It just ain't any longer!"

He winked at her and drove away, laughing loudly.

Eva went back to the house, stomping the snow. She didn't like that story any better than "Mary Morry." Grown-ups laughed at strange things.

Back upstairs she went again. How she missed her friends in Philadelphia. . . . What could she do to-day? She had already explored the house from top to bottom. And it was goose-pimply cold outside—no fun to go down and poke around the barn. It wasn't a very good morning. Maybe "Wonderland" would help.

onderland

was a big drawer in her mother's tall bureau that held all kinds of treasures. Eva never grew tired of looking through them.

Climbing on a chair, she pulled at the heavy drawer. Slowly it opened far enough for her to reach inside. Eva lifted out the white bonnet she had worn as a baby and stuck it on her head. It looked so silly and small and floppy that she giggled at herself in the mirror.

Next she emptied the bag of coins and counted them: the odd two-cent pieces almost as big as quarters, the Indian head pennies, the big shiny silver dollars, and one gold piece marked five dollars. How could it be only the size of a nickel and worth that much? She stacked the coins neatly in piles.

Then she picked up the heavy old bullet that her father had found on the battlefield at Gettysburg when he was a boy. It had been his most favorite prize. Though it was only an empty shell, Eva held it gingerly. She never liked the feel of it. She looked for a place to hide it.

Reaching far into the corner of the drawer to tuck the bullet away, Eva felt something hard and strange. She was puzzled. She thought she knew everything in the Wonderland drawer. Eagerly she moved aside the homespun linen towels to see what it could be.

Great Granny's old tin box with the gay painted flowers!

In Philadelphia the box had sat on the highest shelf in the closet. How many times had she looked up at it, wondering if something might be hidden in it? Even standing on a chair she had never been able to reach it. Now, right this minute, she was going to find out. She set the box down on the floor.

Lifting the lid carefully, Eva peeked inside. There *was* something. But what? A bunch of thin metal pieces packed close together. She made a wry face. "Scraps! Nothing but scraps of old tin! I was so sure there'd be treasure in Great Granny's box!"

Eva was about to shut the box in disgust when suddenly she decided to look and see if something might be hidden in the bottom. She worked out one piece of tin, then another and another. Her eyes grew brighter and her smile grew wider as she spread them in front of her. They were cookie cutters.

But such cookie cutters! Here was a man riding a horse, there a big proud rooster, here his hen. There were birds, lot of birds. One had a funny round tail— could it be a peacock? Two were joined together at the breast, looking into each other's eyes. Eva held that one the longest. And there was the funniest little man, a tiny camel, and a tulip.

Eva gathered them and ran downstairs to her mother. "Look what I found," she cried.

Mrs. Moyer's eyes opened wide. "Where in the world did you get those?"

"In Great Granny's old tin box. Up in Wonderland."

Mrs. Moyer lifted a cookie cutter and looked at it long and lovingly. "They remind me of one Christmas when I was a girl and Great Granny was living with us," she said. "Evie, I will tell you a *real* story."

"Goody!" Eva sat down on the rug. "At last!"

"That Christmas," Mrs. Moyer began, "I was just about your age. My sister Hilda was five years older and she thought she was all grown-up. She told our mother that we girls had decided we were too big to have a Christmas tree."

"Did you agree with her, Mom?" Eva couldn't believe it.

"No!" Mrs. Moyer shook her head. "But I was so shocked when I heard her say it that I didn't speak up in time. So the tree was never ordered from the farmer.

"Great Granny," she went on, "had a way of coming to the rescue when little girls were upset. She showed me these cookie cutters. She told me how, in the old days, folks decorated trees with cookies. That gave me the idea. I could make a cookie tree, and we would have a Christmas tree in spite of Hilda.

"So I kept it a secret from her," Mrs. Moyer said. "I baked when Mother baked and decorated the cookies when Hilda went out on errands."

"But where did you get a tree," Eva asked, "if it was too late to get one from the farmer?"

"I found a tiny evergreen in the bushes in back of the yard," Mrs. Moyer answered. "I cut it down when nobody was looking. Then I hung my cookies on it. I hid the cookie tree in the granary, a little room in the barn where Father stored the oats for the horses.

"On Christmas morning," Mrs. Moyer said, "I flew down to the barn to get my surprise. When I opened the door to the granary, I was the one who got the surprise! There was not—one—single—cookie on my tree!"

Eva was horrified. "What happened to them, Mom?"

"It took me just one minute to figure it out, Evie," her mother said, "I looked around for some trace of the cookies, and I spied a little hole near the door. Mice! The mice had eaten every last one. Not even a crumb was left."

"Oh, that's a sad story," Eva said.

"Yes," Mrs. Moyer nodded. "And I cried. I was still

crying when Hilda found me. I sobbed out the story, and she hugged me and dried my tears. She said she was sorry about my cookies and sorry about not having a Christmas tree. We took the poor bare tree back to the house and into the parlor. There we hung our own gifts on it. And, believe me, Evie, never again did anyone say that we were too big to have a Christmas tree!"

"But I bet that tree went down in Mouse History," Eva said.

Mrs. Moyer laughed. "Maybe so!"

"Mommie!" Eva jumped up. "Could I make a cookie tree?"

Soon the kitchen smelled of sugar and spice and Christmas. Eva and her mother mixed, rolled, and cut with the old cookie cutters. In each cookie they made a little hole for the string to go through.

The first pan of cookies came from the oven. The little hen was round and plump. The proud rooster puffed out his chest. The double birds touched their bills together.

Mrs. Moyer lifted the funniest little man and gave him to Eva. "Now make a wish," she said. "When you eat something for the first time in a season, make a wish, and your wish will come true."

It wasn't hard for Eva to decide what she wanted most. She didn't wish for games. She didn't wish for clothes or a book. She wished for something far more important. "I wish—" she started to say, but her mother stopped her.

"Wait! Don't tell your wish to anyone! That would spoil it."

Eva closed her mouth and made the wish to herself.

Mrs. Moyer picked up the mixing bowl and scraped it clean. "Give me all your snipples, Evie," she said.

Eva handed her the pieces left over from cutting out the cookies.

"We won't waste any." Her mother made a ball

from the last bits of sweet-smelling dough. "Great Granny always said, 'The cook can throw out more with her spoon than her man can bring in with a shovel.' "

Eva giggled. She could just picture her father bringing in flour and sugar and spices on his shovel. And her mother throwing it all out the back door with a spoon.

Taking the ball of dough made from the snipples, Eva rolled it flat. Carefully and firmly she pressed down the horse and rider. As she picked up the cutter, her mouth fell open. "Oh, Mom! Look what happened! The horse lost his leg!"

"It's only stuck in the cutter." Mrs. Moyer handed her a small knife. "Just lift the leg out and put it back on the horse."

Eva worked the broken leg onto the horse, wetting her finger to smooth the joint. It was almost as good as new. She gave the leg a little twist backward. The horse was galloping!

A faint, burning odor came from the stove. "Uh-oh," cried Mrs. Moyer, running to the oven and snatching out the pan of cookies. "We'd better keep our minds on our business," she said, looking ruefully at the blackened shapes. "Oh well," she brightened, "a little charcoal is good for the stomach."

Eva rolled her eyes. "Ugh! My tummy likes gingerbread better!"

"But birds might like them," her mother said. "Why don't you take the burned cookies out to them? Birds have a hard time finding food when snow is on the ground."

Eva crumbled the burned cookies and threw handfuls of crumbs under the horse chestnut tree. The birds up on the branches watched anxiously. But they stayed in the tree.

Eva stepped back and stood still as a statue.

A cocky blue jay made the first move. He swooped down, picked up the biggest crumb and flew swiftly away. Several little chickadees dropped like stones to the snow and started to feed. With their feathers puffed out to keep them warm, they were round balls of fluff.

Eva kept very still, her eyes on a bright red cardinal. Cautiously he dropped from branch to branch, pausing on each one to cock his eye at Eva. At last he flew down, landing a safe distance away from the crumbs. He hopped slowly over to investigate them. He picked up one crumb and found it to his liking. His head bobbed up and down as he gobbled them greedily.

Just like bobbing for apples on Halloween, Eva thought.

Up on her perch, his timid mate hesitated. Eva held her breath. Would she come down too? Abruptly, with a flutter of wings, the brown cardinal landed beside the red one. She pecked hungrily, nervously, her head held to one side, watching Eva.

From the corner of her eye, Eva caught a flash of red on the tree trunk. The redheaded woodpecker was coming down backwards! He hopped off the tree and over to the crumbs. Choosing a large piece, he flew with it in his beak back to the tree. There he wedged the crumb into the bark. With his wirelike feet clinging to the bark, he picked at his find.

Eva thought that a very tidy way to eat.

Soon sparrows, starlings, and juncoes appeared out of nowhere. Eva had never seen so many birds—nor so close, except for the pigeons she used to feed in the park in Philadelphia.

The crumbs were almost gone. Cold and tired of standing still so long, Eva moved her foot. The startled birds flew away, and Eva hopped back to the house, back to her baking.

When the pile of cookies had grown quite large, Mrs. Moyer set out a box of confectioner's sugar. "We had better ice some cookies now, Evie," she said. "They'll have to dry overnight before we can put colors on them. Otherwise the colors will run into the white coating, and we'll be in trouble."

Following her mother's directions, Eva mixed a thin white icing about the thickness of pancake batter. This she spread on the cookies with a flat butter knife. She set them aside near the stove to dry.

The next morning the icing was hard and shining. Eva mixed a new batch. She put out four small bowls and divided the icing among them. To each bowl she added drops of food coloring—red, yellow, blue, green. These she mixed. The most wonderful of wonderful colors appeared.

She took a small paintbrush and loaded it with blue icing.

Mrs. Moyer said, "Now hold your brush straight up and down. Touch just the tip of it to the cookie. Pull your brush up fast, and what do you have?"

"An eye!—Buttons!" Eva cried, looking at the fat round dot with delight. "And polka dots! Polka dots will be great for birds!"

"Now we'll make petals and feathers. Watch me." Mrs. Moyer loaded the brush with red.

"Hold your brush as if you were going to paint. Push down on your brush at the beginning of your stroke. Slowly lift it up as you pull the brush away from you. See, round and thick at the beginning. Thin and fine at the end."

Eva tried. Then she frowned. Somehow her stroke didn't look at all like her mother's.

"Keep at it," Mrs. Moyer said. "You'll get better as you go along."

Soon the proud rooster spread his big tail of many colors. His little hen sat contentedly on her eggs. The peacock's round tail glowed like jewels. The tulip burst into bloom.

Eva was so pleased with the gay, bright cookies that she felt she would burst if she didn't tell someone about them.

Early the next morning, out by the mailbox, she told the mailman in a rush of excited words.

"Now ain't that just wonderful nice, Dutchess." Mr. Dietrich smiled at her. "Whoever heard tell of such a thing!"

Eva raced back to the house. She hadn't done the man on the horse yet. He could have a bright blue coat. . . . And the double birds, she could put lots of color on them, like the lovebirds she had seen at the Philadelphia zoo. There was so *much* to do if her tree was to have lots of cookies. She went right to the kitchen and set out her bowls of icings.

Tray after tray Eva filled with gay painted cookies. Each finished trayful seemed prettier than the last.

Mr. Moyer came into the kitchen, his ax over his shoulder and a rope coiled in his hand. He sniffed the mouth-watering smells. "That's what I call Christmas," he said. "Molasses and ginger — cinnamon and nutmeg." He admired the horse and rider. He popped a cookie into his mouth. "I know an old saying, too." He looked at his wife. " 'A hungry mouth needs no coaxing.' Think Great Granny might have said that, Mary?" He turned to wink at Eva. Eva snickered.

Mrs. Moyer smiled at him, crinkling her eyes. "She might've, Dan, she might've."

"Your Great Granny sure must have been related to Ben Franklin." Mr. Moyer gobbled another cookie. "He had a saying for everything, too. Well, anyway, you women have stuck together long enough now." He walked toward the door. "Come on, Puss. Get your wraps. I have something to show you."

Eva jumped up quickly, upsetting the bowl of red icing. It spattered on the table, on the floor, on her father.

"What a *dopple* you are!" Mr. Moyer scolded, rubbing a spot of red icing off his sleeve. "Look at that mess! Get a washrag and clean it up and let's go!"

Eva scurried to wipe up the spilled icing.

As she tugged on her boots, her father snitched one last cookie. Then they went out the door.

They walked past the barn and into the woods. Mr. Moyer led Eva to the youngest, prettiest, roundest pine tree. "Think this will do for your cookies, Snicklefritz?" he asked.

"Oh, Daddy, it's just right!" Eva hugged him.

Her father chopped it down. Then they picked out a

larger tree to put in the living room. Mr. Moyer cut that down and tied a rope around the trunk. He dragged it through the snow back to the house, Eva dancing gaily ahead of him, carrying her own little tree.

The next morning Eva put the strings in the cookies. She was as busy as a hen with a brood of new chicks, so busy that she even forgot about the mailman until she heard the honk of his horn. She flew out of the house to meet him.

"*Ich hab* a present—I have a present for you, Dutchess." Mr. Dietrich held out to her three more old cookie cutters. An angel, a hissing goose, and a star. "I thought you might like these yet for your *Grishdawg* tree."

"*Grishdawg* tree?" she asked.

"Your *Christmas* tree," he explained.

"Oh, *donk ya!*" Eva cried.

Mr. Dietrich chuckled. "Dutchess," he said, "you just talked Dutch, all by yourself!"

Eva cut out one more batch of cookies with the mailman's gift. The star she put on the top of the tree, where stars belong.

The day before Christmas she waited at the mailbox. When the mailman came, she begged him, "Please come in for just one little minute, Mr. Dietrich. My tree's all finished."

"*Yah gewiss*, yes indeed! You bet your life I sure would like to see that tree!" He followed her quickly into the house, his face beaming.

On the table stood the small tree, loaded with cookies, sparkling with colors. Mr. Dietrich walked up to it and stood still. He took off his hat. He looked. . . . And he looked. He touched the shining rooster, the glistening peacock.

"*Shana, shana,*" he whistled softly, "it gives such a beautiful tree, Dutchess. It pretties up the place so." He took Eva's hand in his. "It pities me yet to think the

whole world can't see it. That just ain't right!''

It was Christmas Eve at last. Eva sat at the table before her tree, admiring it.

''It's a much prettier tree than the one I made,'' Mrs. Moyer said. ''But you'd better go now and put on your Sunday best. Before we know it, it'll be time for the Christmas program at the church.''

''Do I have to go, Mommie?'' Eva asked in a low voice. Her happy feeling disappeared.

''Certainly you have to go,'' her mother replied crisply.

''But, Mom, I *can't!*'' Eva wailed, suddenly remembering. ''I forgot! I have to bring a present, and I don't have one!''

''A present?'' her mother asked.

''Yes,'' Eva said, ''it's part of the program—to give a present to the baby Jesus.''

Mrs. Moyer looked perplexed. "Well, there must be something around here that you can wrap and take. You think about it while I'm getting supper."

Eva sat in the back seat of the car as they drove down the winding road to the church. She was too excited to talk. Mr. and Mrs. Moyer were silent, lost in their own thoughts.

They turned into the church yard. The bell in the steeple was pealing. Christmas lights streamed bright and friendly from the tall windows. Laughing, chattering people visited gaily in small groups outside the door. The air was crisp and festive.

Mr. Moyer helped Eva carry her gift into the church basement.

All at once Eva felt afraid. "Do you think the children will laugh at my gift?" she whispered to her father.

"Of course not," he whispered back. "Now don't you worry, Puss. They'll love it."

They went up the crooked stairs to the little room next to the altar, where the children were getting ready. Eva's father patted her on the shoulder and disappeared out into the buzzing crowd of people beyond the door. Eva stood alone with her gift. All the boys and girls were looking at her now with eyes and mouths like big round O's of astonishment.

The lights dimmed. The church was hushed. To the back room came the echo of the minister's opening prayer, and the bursting forth of the glad Christmas carols. The older children, dressed in flowing robes, left to go out to the front of the church for the Nativity scene. Mary, proud with love. Humble Joseph. The lowly shepherds, and the Wise Men with their hand-

some gifts. A strong, young voice read the Christmas story.

When the words of the carol "We Three Kings of Orient Are" drifted in, Eva saw the minister's wife give the signal to the waiting children. One by one they filed in and laid down their gifts before the manger. Eva was last.

Carrying her gift, she walked slowly and carefully through the door, her heart pounding. Out there in the half-darkness the people sat to watch—the Pennsylvania Dutch neighbors whom she didn't know. She could hear their quick gasps of breath when they saw her gift. "Ai! Ah! Ai!" they whispered in wonderment.

It was her cookie tree. It was the gift of her heart.

Eva joined the row of children. They smiled at her now as if they had one face. Together they all said,

"What shall I give Him, poor as I am?
If I were a shepherd, I'd give Him a lamb.
If I were a Wise Man, I'd do my part.
Yet what shall I give Him? Give Him my heart."

The girl with the nice face and the lively brown eyes reached over and took Eva's hand. She gave it a warm squeeze and said softly, "We live neighbors. I take you to school next week."

Eva thought she would burst with happiness. They did like her tree. And she would have a friend! The wish she had made on that first cookie was coming true. No longer would she be a stranger. Dimly she could see her mother's and father's happy faces. And way in the back she spied Mr. Dietrich, smiling.

Late that night when Eva was about to crawl into bed she heard voices outside. She rushed to the window and looked out. A group of people stood caroling under the big horse chestnut tree. Her nose pressed flat against the icy pane, she listened and watched.

At the end of the singing, the carolers called out "Merry Christmas!" at the top of their voices. Then they shouted an old Pennsylvania Dutch New Year's wish. Only they shouted it in English so the *Auslanders* could understand it.

"We wish you a happy New Year!
A pretzel like a barn door—
A sausage like a stove pipe
As long as from here to Baltimore!"

Then swinging their lanterns, laughing and singing, they left.

Eva hopped on one foot to her bed. She snuggled down under the covers. And tomorrow it will be Christmas, she thought sleepily.

. . . My first . . . happy *Grishdawg* . . . day . . .

MAKE A COOKIE TREE OR COOKIE PRESENTS

Patterns

If you do not have cookie cutters, draw your own designs or trace Eva's. Cut out tracing and paste on thin cardboard. Cut out cardboard pattern, and lay it on the rolled-out dough. Carefully and firmly cut around the pattern with a knife.

Great Granny's Gingerbread Recipe

1 cup butter   4 cups flour
1 cup molasses   1 teaspoon soda
1 cup light brown sugar   ½ teaspoon salt
Spices: 2 teaspoons ginger, 1 teaspoon cinnamon, 1 teaspoon nutmeg, ¼ teaspoon each of mace, cloves, and allspice.

Melt butter, add sugar and molasses. Sift together, into a large bowl, flour, soda, salt, and spices. Blend in melted butter, molasses, and sugar. Chill the dough for an hour. Place a piece of chilled dough on a floured surface and roll out to about ⅛" thickness. Cut out cookies and place on baking sheet. If you plan to put them on the tree, make holes for hanging them.

Bake at 350° for about ten minutes. Small cookies may take less time.

Icing

1 box confectioner's sugar
3 to 4 tablespoons water
food colors
small watercolor brushes—1 for each color

Stir 3 tablespoons of water into sugar. Add more as necessary to make it the thickness of pancake batter. Divide icing into cups. Add desired color to each cup.

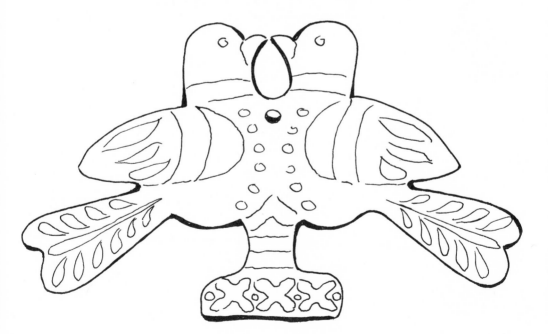

Tree Ornaments—"Just for Nice"

1 cup salt
4 cups flour
1½ cups water

Mix flour and salt together. Pour water slowly into flour and salt, mixing constantly. Knead this dough for ten minutes. Sprinkle rolling surface with flour. Roll dough to ¼"—thicker than regular cookies. Cut out cookies. Pull dough away from cutters. Place cookies on baking sheet and make holes in cookies for hanging them.

Bake in slow oven 275° for about one and a half hours. Cookies will be hard and a light-brown color when done.

Decorate these "permanent cookies" with acrylic paints. *Do not let your friends try to eat them!*

Decorating

Colorful cookies can be made without first coating them with white icing as Eva did. Simply paint directly on the cookie. Use white icing as one of the decorating colors. It shows up well on the brown gingerbread.

For the "permanent cookies," you may still want to use the white coating first. Acrylic paint dries quickly. Use a larger brush to coat cookies, front and edges. When dry, coat the back. The white coating makes them very showy on the tree.

Follow the decorating directions that Eva's mother gave her. Add your own imagination. The Pennsylvania Dutch did.

WHO ARE THE PENNSYLVANIA DUTCH?

The first Pennsylvania Dutch came to eastern Pennsylvania from Germany and Switzerland as early as 1683. They left their homeland because of many years of war and religious quarrels.

These German-speaking peoples were called Pennsylvania "Dutch" because the English settlers mispronounced *Deutsch*—the word for "German"—as "Dutch."

The early Pennsylvania Dutchmen loved color and design. Thrifty and hardworking, they made everything they used, and decorated much of it with hearts, tulips, angels, stars, and birds. Pennsylvania Folk Art, as it is now called, is a rich gift they left to all America.

The Pennsylvania Dutch are divided into two groups—"Plain" and "Fancy." Because of their strong religious beliefs, some of the "Plain People" still wear old-fashioned clothes and live as their forefathers did. The "Plain People" are the Amish, Mennonites, and Brethren. They settled in Lancaster, York, and Montgomery counties.

By far the larger group, the "Fancy Dutch" loved

life and believed that religion, home, and family were of equal importance. They settled in Berks, Lehigh, Northampton, Lebanon, and Dauphin counties.

The "Fancy Dutch" started many American Christmas customs. The "Christ-Child" brought gifts to their children before Santa Claus was known. The first Christmas trees appeared in country Dutch homes. And the Dutch housewife baked Christmas cookies by the washbasketful.

As one writer of the Pennsylvania Dutch people has said, "If the Puritans were the soul of America, the Pennsylvania Dutch were surely its heart."